Juliette Gordon Low wears a 1912-1919 nainsook princess slip. The top of the corset cover and the skirt flounce are richly embroidered. Silk satin ribbon runs through beading at the neckline and waistline.

Pat (15-17 years) wears a 1918 corset cover and drawer combination of soft-finished muslin, trimmed with lace and silk satin ribbon.

Lou Henry Hoover wears a 1920 flesh-colored silk crepe de chine envelope chemise, trimmed with insertions and edgings of lace and silk satin ribbon. Soft shirring on midriff area.

Melissa (10-12 years) wears a 1912 girls corset waist with light, flexible boning, button closure in front, lace-up back, and four hose supporters. Her cotton petticoat has eyelet embroidery trim on bottom flounce.

From Melissa's Diary

March 12, 1912: The most incredibly exciting thing has happened—I'm a Girl Guide! I will have a uniform, and earn badges, and go camping, and play basketball in bloomers, and be a much, much better person than I have ever been before. My friend Doots's Aunt Daisy (Juliette Gordon) Low invited those of us who have been doing nature study with Mr. Hoxie to come to tea at the Gordon home, and she told us all about the organization. I wore my new white lawn "tea dress." (Mama said that Girl Guides must be a good thing if Mrs. Low is part of it. Her family has always been well thought of here in Savannah.)

It is just TOO bad that Doots couldn't be here for the investiture ceremony today, when we solemnly said our Girl Guide Promise ("I promise, on my honor—to be loyal to God and my country, to try and do daily good turns to other people, to obey the law of the Guides"), but Miss Daisy (she said we could call her that as we are all sisters in Girl Guiding) wrote Doots's name down the very first on the list! She will be really surprised when Miss Daisy goes out to Myrtle Grove plantation and tells her about all that is happening.

The first time we met with Miss Daisy, she told us how we are to carry on the heritage of the knights of old by doing a good turn every day. Every morning we are to tie a knot in our neckerchief as a reminder, untying it after the good turn is done. I find this is a very good thing to do. It quite puts one in a good spirit, and brings a smile to both giver and receiver. I really must stop writing now, dear Diary, so I will have time to study my whistle signals. I WILL "Be Prepared" (that's our motto) at our next meeting, by knowing every single one of them.

May 27, 1912: Doots loves being a Girl Guide as much as I do! She has always been proud of being named for her wonderful Aunt Daisy, even though her family nicknamed her Doots—I think it is a variation on "deuce" (another word for "two")—to avoid the confusion of having two "Daisy's" in the family. Girl Guiding is simply glorious, and as it is becoming ever more popular—and popu*lous* (wouldn't my English grammar teacher just LOVE that piece of usage!), I secretly suspect Miss Doots Gordon will only become MORE proud to be named for Mrs. Daisy Gordon Low!

Yesterday we pretended not to know one another on the street so that we could give the secret sign of holding up three fingers, and then use the Guides' secret passwords which we have learned in preparation for our Second Class test. I asked her, "D neir felt til," and she properly responded, "deraper peb." Then I asked, "lortap ruoysi tahuu?" and she said, "White Carnation." We learned a lot reading the Girl Guide book that Doots's aunt gave her, hunting for each hidden password written in it. We were proud of ourselves for thinking to read the secret passwords backward, and for realizing on the last one that "uu" was for "double-u" or the letter "w." We have mastered the whistle signals, and are now hard at work on semaphore! As soon as we earn the Second Class

rank, we can begin working on tests for proficiency badges.

We were very impressed to read the paragraph on "When to Wear the Badge." It tells us Girl Guides, "You can wear your trefoil badge any day and any hour when you are doing what you think is right. It is only when you are doing wrong that you must take it off; as you would not then be keeping your Guide promises. Thus you should either take off the Badge, or stop doing what you think is wrong." We shall strive always to remember this good advice.

I have learned to use Mama's sewing machine and made my very own Girl Guide uniform. It is a middy blouse and skirt of dark blue duck, with a light blue sateen tie. It seems that every girl who sees us in our uniforms wants to join us! Miss Daisy has given us the use of the old carriage house at the back of the Low property, and has put a sign on it showing that it is Girl Guide headquarters. She is setting up a basketball court and tennis court for us on a vacant lot across from the Low house. It's only practical to play in our bloomers, so we will wear our coats over them from headquarters until we get inside the screening around the lot. We do not wish to be thought immodest.

May 1, 1913: So much has happened since I last wrote about my Girl Scouts (we are beginning to call ourselves this instead of Girl Guides). We have held an entertainment for our mothers, and there is now a weekly column about us in the Savannah *Morning News!*

Miss Daisy has been back and forth to England, bringing more books and badges, which were most welcome! My Second Class badge was one of them. I very carefully sewed it onto the left sleeve of my uniform. I think the hardest—and the best—thing I did to earn my Second Class badge was making the United States flag. Making that flag made me think of Betsy Ross making the first one. She only put on thirteen stars; since New Mexico and Arizona became states last year there are forty-eight for me to sew on. I am working especially hard to earn my First Class rank. I have earned Clerk (I thought I should NEVER master the typewriter, but Granddaddy was very patient about coming down to his architecture office at night to let me get in extra practice on his typewriter there), Cook (Papa was very pleased with my progress on this—especially as I learned to be more frugal, and even my brothers Kevin, Allan, and Steve were complimentary of my Irish stew and rice pudding), Musician, Child Nurse, and Naturalist (those of us who have worked so long with Mr. Hoxie were determined to finish this one with flying colors, so he could be proud of his pupils). Miss Daisy says patrols and companies are springing up everywhere. While she was gone, she arranged for some of her friends to take us driving, and on her return she purchased a launch which we have delighted in using on the Savannah River. Several of us have hopes of earning our Boatswain badge. But best of all, she took all of us who were in the first two patrols on a five-day camping trip! We had such a wonderful time! Around the campfire at night, Daisy Low read our palms (she said she had been doing this for years and thought it great fun), shared some of the tales about Boy Scouts and

Girl Guides in England as told to her by her great friend Sir Baden-Powell, told us about some of the fun she and her cousins had growing up (including the time Page Anderson's papa braided taffy into Daisy's hair!), and about her ancestress Eleanor Lytle Kinzie. Eleanor (called Nelly) actually lived with the Indians in Illinois for several years after they captured her at the age of nine. The Indians gave her a nickname exemplifying her great and unyielding determination, which Miss Daisy admitted her family has given to her as well (and for the same reason!), that of "Little-Ship-under-Full-Sail." The chief, Cornplanter, came to love her as a sister, and finally returned her to her family many years later only because he so wanted HER happiness, not just his own. Miss Daisy said all the Kinzies AND Sir Baden-Powell would be proud of the way we camped, including the fact that our food only cost us eleven cents a day! After this trip, we all agreed that our vote to change our uniform color to khaki was a very good idea. Red Georgia soil and blue uniforms are not at all complementary to one another!

Daisy Low never stops doing great things for us. She and Mr. Hoxie are working very hard on a handbook, so we in America can have one of our very own. She told us it will be published later this year. Isn't that exciting? Another source of excitement around our house is my cousin Sheila's wedding next week! I will be her junior bridesmaid. My dress has yards and yards of lace and a pink underslip. My hat (truly sophisticated!) is silk braid, lace, and pale pink chiffon with ribbon trim.

August 15, 1915: I'm a Corporal! Earning my First Class badge was SO exciting, but this is every bit as good! I have just sewn the Corporal's stripe onto the left sleeve of my uniform, just above my First Class badge. My Patrol Leader, Sharon, says she will be relying on me to help her a lot. I feel very keenly the weight of this responsibility. When I help at the next investiture by handing the new girl her staff, and putting on her hat, neckerchief, and shoulder knot, I will listen in a different way than ever before as the Captain tells her that her trefoil badge is her "life." I will know that the Captain is putting her trust in Sharon and me to help train her, so that her "life" may not be taken away for misbehavior, causing her to "lose her Girl Scout life" for that day or week.

Our Captain says she wants the Patrol Leaders and Corporals to be responsible for most of the planning and teaching of our patrols, so I am re-reading the handbook from cover to cover, making plans. Two all-time favorites are how to secure a burglar with eight inches of cord, and making a star umbrella to help with teaching the constellations and direction-finding. I will make certain each new girl learns how to perform Empress Eugenie's circle. (This is done by walking in a tight circle with right shoulders to the center, and on signal, bending to sit on the knees of the girl behind you. It sounds impossible, but is in truth a wonderful way to rest without soiling one's uniform on the ground or the damp. Perhaps even more importantly, it teaches trust among the girls.) As I love birds as much as Miss Daisy does (Doots has told me that Miss Daisy had a mockingbird sent to her home in England to keep her company), we will work hard on bird identification. I also want to read Rudyard Kipling's story

of Kim to them and then let them play Kim's game. (Miss Daisy loves to tell of "stunts" she and her dear friend Mr. Kipling have pulled!)

Our company has been lending our tents to other patrols, but the captain of another company in town has said that they want to begin paying us rental on them, as that is one way our handbook suggests a patrol might make money. I think we will try another handbook suggestion this winter and make our own tents. There are lots of other suggestions we may use, too, like all the things to make from a brick, and one of Miss Daisy's favorite ideas—putting on a play. We shall use the funds we earn to help purchase food for some of the town's poor at Christmas, just as we are now using the produce of our patrol garden to give to them. There is so much good we can do—the more we learn, the more we can help others!

Miss Daisy comes to visit us often, and tells us how Girl Scouting is progressing nationally. We were so proud when the trefoil design was officially patented last year, and of course we were glad that Daisy Low was elected the first president of the newly incorporated organization this year. Mama says that Miss Daisy sold her beautiful pearls earlier this year to provide money to keep everything running. Miss Daisy is back in England now, trying to help her friends and family who are in jeopardy because of the war. She writes that Girl Guides are doing wonderful deeds to help their country during this desperate time.

November 12, 1918: It's just the best news imaginable—the Armistice has been signed and the war is officially over at last! Miss Daisy is so proud of the work all her Girl Scouts have done across the nation to help with the war effort. As soon as the War Service Award was introduced in our Girl Scout magazine, *The Rally,* last March, many, many girls began working to earn the points necessary to receive the award. The girls in MY patrol (yes, I am just finishing my year as Patrol Leader!) have knitted items to give to the Red Cross (we were amazed when we realized just how much time and effort is required to knit up two pounds of wool, but as we imagined our own brothers sitting in France with cold, wet feet, our needles began flying faster and faster), and several managed to preserve the required fifty containers of jelly or jam this past summer. Georgia peaches DO make the BEST! Of course we saved the peach pits as everyone around the country does, to help in the production of gas masks. Backyard gardens have sprung up everywhere—I heard from Pat that the Girl Scouts in Boston even planted beans on the Common! Girl Scouts helped in Red Cross sewing rooms and in canteens set up in railway stations. We had a drive to sell Liberty Bonds to all the families we know. Through it all, we have been doing just as we have been taught in Girl Scouts—economizing, although now, in honor of Mr. Hoover, who is running the U. S. Food Administration, we say we will "Hooverize" instead.

I just realized that I haven't yet written about my new friend, Pat, who is a Girl Scout in New York. I met her last summer when she came to visit her grandmother here in Savannah. While she was sightseeing, she spotted me in my uniform walking to our troop meeting. She spoke, and we exchanged introductions and Girl Scout handshakes. We thoroughly enjoyed sharing our experiences, talking about everything from badges to armbands. Her patrol chose the Purple Pansy Patrol Crest, and bought several armbands to keep on hand for new members to wear until they can get their uniforms—a very good idea, I think! We decided then and there to become Girl Scout pen pals. The "garden-on-the-Common" project was reported to her by her own Girl Scout cousin in Boston.

Miss Daisy planned a wonderful reunion last month at Myrtle Grove for all of us "original" Girl Scouts. At our reunion, evening campfires were favorite times, as always. In addition to repeating all our favorite tales, Daisy Low talked about her pride in this great movement of ours. Just imagine the thrill she experienced last year when the wife of the President of the United States, Mrs. Woodrow Wilson, became Girl Scouts' first Honorary President. Miss Daisy said she hopes this will establish a tradition for years to come.

I felt very sentimental about Juliette Low—we all did. It was both great fun AND a great trial to be around her so much without giving away the secret of the gift we know is to be presented to her at the National Conference and Rally next May in Washington, D.C.

When we lovingly teased Miss Daisy about some of the "quaint" ways she has of spelling certain words in her frequent letters to us, she freely admitted her lifelong difficulties with spelling. She told us that when she was away at school as a young girl, her mother used to correct the spelling in the letters Miss Daisy sent home! She laughed as she told us this, but laughed even harder remembering the time SHE caught her MOTHER in a spelling error in one of her letters! Her mother had spelled "balance" with two "l's," and Miss Daisy wrote back saying that she never used the word herself as she never HAD any balance, either in her bank or in her actions! We all laughed so hard we cried. We had no sooner recovered from this anecdote than she told us about the time the national Executive Committee was having a meeting and one of the agenda items was the selection of shoes for girls. Mrs. Helen Storrow gave Miss Daisy a pair of the shoes under consideration to wear for the day. When it came time for the discussion, Mrs. Anne Hyde Choate asked Miss Daisy to show them off. She did so by first decorously tucking her skirts firmly between her legs and then standing on her head and waving the shoes in the air! It seems impossible to be around Miss Daisy without laughing. Doots and I found a whole page about laughing and smiling in the first Girl Guide handbook. We still remember the quote: "Want of laughter means want of health. Laugh as much as you can; it does you good. So when you get a good laugh, laugh on." To turn really serious-minded for a moment, I deeply believe the world needs more of both—more women like Juliette Gordon Low AND more laughter.

Excitement positively radiated from Miss Daisy as she told us about *The Golden Eaglet*, the new film about Girl Scouts which has just been completed. The award the film is named for is a great honor to receive, representing such a wealth of knowledge acquired, good habits formed, and ideals met. As Miss Daisy talked, it was evident that she had her usual great fun during the making of it! The film

is to premier in New York City on January 16, 1919, the day the Fourth Girl Scout National Council Meeting opens there. We are anxious for it to be shown here in Savannah. (Doots and I can hardly wait to see if Miss Daisy will be wearing BOTH her knife and cup on her belt in the film. She has told us often about her grandmother Juliette Kenzie never being without either on her horseback trip to Chicago in 1830. Miss Daisy now considers them part of her uniform, along with her ever-present whistle.)

Miss Daisy also told us about the rapidly growing interest in Girl Scouting for younger and younger girls. The handbook has said that in "special cases" girls younger than ten could become a Junior Tenderfoot in a separate patrol, but now the idea of a group called Brownies is being experimented with. Miss Daisy said she thinks the first pack was formed in Massachusetts in the summer of 1916. There seem to be lots of ideas as to what their uniform should be. I wonder if some day I will have a daughter who will be a Brownie? I hope so.

More excitement! Miss Daisy drew us sketches of the new uniform which will be coming out next month. It looks very stylish, and I especially like the hat! It will take me hours and hours to transfer my insignia, I know, but I am like every other girl in the world—I love new clothes! And do you know—I think I am very much like Miss Daisy in that we both truly love our uniforms.

In addition to our usual laughing, singing, eating, and reminiscing at the reunion, there were two serious topics of discussion: women's suffrage and prohibition. Congress is debating both issues now, and if they pass as Constitutional Amendments, each will make a big difference in our country. We feel we would be the best prepared women voters around, because as Girl Scouts, we have had lots of practice in becoming informed and then making democratic, majority-ruled decisions.

June 15, 1919: The secret is out! At the National Conference and Rally held in Washington, D.C., last month in honor of the visit of Sir Robert and Lady Olave Baden-Powell, our beloved Miss Daisy received a jeweled Thanks badge purchased with pennies given by Girl Scouts from all around the country! It was so good to get to do something for HER for a change—she has given all of us so very much! Sir Robert and Lady Baden-Powell also presented her the Silver Fish Award on behalf of all the British Girl Guides. The award is so named as a "sign for one who makes her way successfully against the stream of difficulties in life." How appropriate for our Daisy Low who has overcome her deafness and all the personal tragedies in her life!

In February, it was decided that the Norfolk uniform jacket is to be designated for officers' wear only. This is the first time there has ever been a difference in the official uniform for girls and officers. We think it is a rather good idea. (Perhaps this is because many of us are now getting old enough to be officers ourselves! Actually, we wish there were something special just for us older girls. Miss Daisy says the idea is being discussed around the country, and that various programs for "Citizen Scouts" and "Senior Girl Scouts" have been proposed.)

And speaking of "propose" . . . my big sister Betty is to be married September 1! Her dress and veil are SO beautiful! Doots and I spent some time this spring re-reading the Girl Guide handbook we first used, before Miss Daisy wrote one just for Girl Scouts. The week Betty announced her engagement, we found in it a discussion of courtesy and politeness which we will remember as rose petals are scattered down the aisle at the wedding. It said that flowers at weddings and other happy occasions show our wish to extend a courtesy, a politeness, a kindness to a friend. Girl Scouts interpret this in their "good turns." My life has been full of the joy of these good turns, given and received, since I joined this Movement.

I know one thing our troop should do the very best of any troop in the city, and that's our drilling. Warren, Betty's fiancé, was a soldier and now he is our drilling instructor for a half hour each week. (He's not only a great instructor, but I personally think he is the kindest and handsomest man I've ever seen! Lucky Betty!)

Pat writes that she has earned her First Class badge and has also been appointed a Patrol Leader! She likes the new uniform as much as I do, too!

February 22, 1920: I have just been appointed a Lieutenant, and have sewn the officer's insignia (a single stripe of black braid for a Lieutenant; two stripes for a Captain) on the left cuff of my uniform! I am both excited and apprehensive. I read back through these notes I have made on my Girl Scout experiences, and remember well the sense of responsibility I felt when I became first a Corporal, then a Patrol Leader. How very much more I know and want to share now, and how much greater is my understanding of the importance and scope of this Movement. I MUST convey this to the girls, and inspire them as I have been inspired!

I have written something very important on my new Girl Scout calendar (the very first one ever published!). At the National Council meeting in Philadelphia in January, Miss Daisy resigned her position as President of the Girl Scouts, and will just hold the title of Founder. Mrs. Anne Hyde Choate is the new President.

Pat wrote a long, chatty letter about her impending graduation in May. She and her mother have been designing her graduation dress, and it sounds lovely. We girls do love our elegant white dresses, don't we? I wrote back and told her she was long overdue for a return visit to Savannah—and me!

My cousin, Erin, who has just joined a patrol, came by last night so she could show us her new uniform. She proudly showed us the wrinkles in the ends of her neckerchief where she had tied knots and then untied them during the day as she did a good turn for someone. (This is not done much anymore, but she had heard Doots and I talk about it so much that she says she is going to do it until she feels she has become what she calls a "real Girl Scout.") As we visited, the idea of her taking over the recording of a young Girl Scout's experiences occurred to us both at the same time. It will be fun to have someone else in the family to talk about Girl Scouting with!

From Erin's Diary

February 22, 1920: I am a Girl Scout just like Melissa now! Well, *nearly* like her; she's lots and lots older than I am and has been a Girl Scout ever since Daisy Low founded them. Her uniform sleeves are FULL of badges, and she has loads of award pins! She has told me about all the things that she has learned, and I am going to work just as hard as Melissa did. Our patrol has selected the bluebonnet for our patrol crest. Maybe it will bring us the luck of someday getting to visit Texas, where the bluebonnet is the state flower!

We should be receiving our new handbook very soon. I think I will probably sit down and read it from cover to cover the minute I get it. I just know it will have so many things in it that I will want to do I will not want to take time for a single thing in my life other than trying new Girl Scout activities! It is to have a khaki-colored cover, to match our uniforms, and will be called *Scouting For Girls.*

Oh, Mother just came in and brought my new issue of *The Rally,* our Girl Scout magazine. I can't wait to read it!

June 5, 1920: What a coincidence! My last entry concerned *The Rally,* and it was this month's issue which sent me here to make an entry. The name has just changed to *The American Girl!* Oh dear, no more time to write—I see it is time for our troop meeting. I must have read longer than I thought!

November 21, 1920: I have worked very hard and have earned my Second Class rank, so I am now working on proficiency badges. I decided to work on Health Winner first, as it is an annual badge. It will be fun to repeat it (except for not eating sweets between meals), and then be able to embroider first a red line, then a white one, and then a blue one around the outside of the badge, to show each time I have re-earned it! It was such a thrill to receive my very first badge, and I worked ever so carefully on making my stitches tiny when I sewed it on. My grandmother, Nonna, was really proud of me. When she was young, girls took pride in their needlework. I think it disappoints her a little that I would rather tramp around in the woods or play basketball than work on a sampler. So I decided it would be a very proper "good turn" if I sewed my badges on in the way she would have. This is a part of what Daisy Low meant when she told us that "the more a Girl Scout does, the more she sees to do."

July 11, 1921: I was absolutely, positively correct about the new handbook. It is full of new badges, new information, new things to do. It has kept me busy indeed!

For part of the test for my Craftsman proficiency badge, I tie-dyed a scarf, which I will give to Nonna for her birthday. I am still working on the china painting requirement for it. Miss Daisy showed us some of the china she has painted, and hers is so beautiful it both inspires and discourages me!

Attendance
1913-1916,
Invalid Cook
1916-1918

Artist
1913-1918

Cyclist
1913-1918

In February 1919, the Norfolk jacket was reserved for adults, the first time uniform distinguished girls from adults. Sir Robert and Lady Olave Baden-Powell presented the English Silver Fish Award to Juliette Low in May 1919. Shoulder cords, hat cords, and pins replaced chevrons as adult position indicators in 1917. The insignia on adults' flat-crowned hats was introduced in 1919.

Afternoon tea dress of silk and satin with embroidery trim. Underwaist of lace-trimmed white chiffon.

Earliest uniform for both girls and adults, varying only in rank insignia. A "summer white" version, approved in 1920, was worn with black or colored tie, khaki hat, and khaki armband. Two chevrons on the left sleeve signified an adult Lieutenant. Patrol crest was worn on the sleeve. Shoulder knot ribbons matched colors of the patrol crest. Adults earned and wore proficiency badges until 1923. The GS hat pin was introduced in 1915.

Dairy Maid
1913-1916,
Dairy 1916-1918

1913
Handbook

Health
1913-1916,
Personal Health
1916-1918

Farmer
1913-1918

1919   JGL

1919

1912

1919   JGL

1919

1915   G·S   B

1912   B

How Girls can Help Their Country

HANDBOOK for Girl Scouts

Boatswain
1916-1918

Swimmer
1916-1918,
Boatswain
1913-1916

Rifle Shot
1913-1916,
Marksmanship
1916-1918

French Gabrielle
afternoon tea
dress of lawn.
Pin-tucks and
Swiss openwork
embroidery on
yoke and on
bretelles
extending to
skirt hem in
front and to
waistline in
back.
Valenciennes
lace edging on
collar and
sleeves.

Tenderfoot
Pin,
1918-1923

Junior
bridesmaid's dress
with skirt, panel,
and cuffs of
imported Swiss
embroidery.
Valenciennes lace
insertions and
edgings on bodice
and cuffs.
Delicate pink silk
ribbon belt, bow,
and princess slip.
Hat of lacy silk
braid in the stylish
mushroom shape.
Plauen lace
around crown and
brim. Ribbon,
bows, and chiffon
lining to match
dress.

Middy and
bloomers for
playing basketball.

Pioneer
1913-1918

Lieutenant's
pin,
1917-1923

Captain's
pin,
1916-1923

Interpreter
1913-1918

Horsemanship
1913-1918

Boatswain
1916-1918

Swimmer
1916-1918,
Boatswain
1913-1916

Rifle Shot
1913-1916,
Marksmanship
1916-1918

French Gabrielle
afternoon tea
dress of lawn.
Pin-tucks and
Swiss openwork
embroidery on
yoke and on
bretelles
extending to
skirt hem in
front and to
waistline in
back.
Valenciennes
lace edging on
collar and
sleeves.

Tenderfoot
Pin,
1918-1923

Junior
bridesmaid's dress
with skirt, panel,
and cuffs of
imported Swiss
embroidery.
Valenciennes lace
insertions and
edgings on bodice
and cuffs.
Delicate pink silk
ribbon belt, bow,
and princess slip.
Hat of lacy silk
braid in the stylish
mushroom shape.
Plauen lace
around crown and
brim. Ribbon,
bows, and chiffon
lining to match
dress.

Middy and
bloomers for
playing basketball.

Pioneer
1913-1918

Lieutenant's
pin,
1917-1923

Captain's
pin,
1916-1923

Interpreter
1913-1918

Horsemanship
1913-1918

Gardening
1918-1920,
Gardener
1920-1926

Laundress
1918-1927

Scribe
1918-1927

Semaphore
signaling was very
popular. Signal
flags were made
either in a diagonal
style or with smaller
squares on
contrasting larger
ones. At the bottom
of Melissa's tie is a
"reminder" knot.
Tied first thing in
the morning, it is
not undone until a
"good turn" has
been done for
someone.

Velvet travel suit with
fur trim and lining
for jacket. Waist area
trimmed with
passementerie, and
tatting in a cloverleaf
pattern. Moiré purse.
(Photo collection, the
Juliette Gordon Low
Girl Scout National
Center, Savannah,
Georgia)

Heavy cotton spring
suit with flower-
trimmed straw hat,
worn on a visit to
Washington, D.C., in
1916. (Photo collec-
tion, the Juliette
Gordon Low Girl Scout
National Center,
Savannah, Georgia)

Golden
Eaglet
Award,
1916-1919

Bugler
1920-1927

Golden
Eaglet
Award,
1919-1939

Zoologist
1920-1927

Beekeeper
1920-1926

Economist
1920-1927

Health
Guardian
1920-1927

Handywoman
1920-1927

High school
graduation dress
of ruffle-trimmed
organdy. Fichu
collar softly
gathered,
crossing at waist
and tying in back
with a large bow.

Shoulder knots were
discontinued in 1919,
and by 1920 girls were
allowed to choose
neckerchief colors. By
1924 a black trefoil was
embroidered on the
point worn in the back.
Certain badges were
worn only on the left
sleeve. Until 1919,
when the First Class
rank was earned, the
Second Class insignia
was removed and sewn
into the center of the
new badge. After 1919,
First Class was embroi-
dered in one piece.
Knot style changed
from four-in-hand to
square knot. Two
chevrons indicate
Patrol Leader.

Everyday dress of
striped percale
cotton with piqué
collar, cuffs, and
patch pockets.
Pearl buttons. Girls
without a uniform
wore an armband.
Patrol crest was
worn between the
GS letters.

Drummer
1920-1927

Community
Service
Award,
1922-1931

War
Service
Award,
1918

Dancer
1920-1925

Dairy Maid
1920-1927

Economist
1920-1927

Health
Guardian
1920-1927

Handywoman
1920-1927

High school
graduation dress
of ruffle-trimmed
organdy. Fichu
collar softly
gathered,
crossing at waist
and tying in back
with a large bow.

Shoulder knots were
discontinued in 1919,
and by 1920 girls were
allowed to choose
neckerchief colors. By
1924 a black trefoil was
embroidered on the
point worn in the back.
Certain badges were
worn only on the left
sleeve. Until 1919,
when the First Class
rank was earned, the
Second Class insignia
was removed and sewn
into the center of the
new badge. After 1919,
First Class was embroi-
dered in one piece.
Knot style changed
from four-in-hand to
square knot. Two
chevrons indicate
Patrol Leader.

Everyday dress of
striped percale
cotton with piqué
collar, cuffs, and
patch pockets.
Pearl buttons. Girls
without a uniform
wore an armband.
Patrol crest was
worn between the
GS letters.

Drummer
1920-1927

Community
Service
Award,
1922-1931

War
Service
Award,
1918

Dancer
1920-1925

Dairy Maid
1920-1927

Business
Woman
1920-1927
shorthand: *Be
Prepared*

Scout Aide
1920-1924

Mrs. Hoover's
colored collar
denotes her status
as National
President. She
served two terms,
1922-1925 and
1935-1937. Between
these terms, she
served as honorary
National President
while her husband
was President of the
United States. Blue
or black collars were
worn by those
serving as
Commissioner or
higher.

Photography
1918-1920,
Photographer
1920-1927

Classic velvet dress
with silver-trimmed
sleeves. Silver and
gold evening
slippers. (From
painting
commissioned by
National Board of
Directors, Girl
Scouts of the U.S.A.,
New York. Courtesy
of Archives,
National Historic
Preservation Center)

Evening gown of
silver metallic
threads woven in
lacelike pattern,
decorated with blue
and cerise glass
beads; fanlike
design. Scarf from
hip. Silver cloth
evening slippers
with slashes over
blue satin.
(Courtesy of the
Herbert Hoover
Presidential
Library-Museum,
West Branch, Iowa)

Horsewoman
1920-1927

Camp
Andree Clark
pin,
1922-1942

Observer
1926-1927

Health Winner
1920-1927

1927 B

1927 B

1927 E

1919 B

1927 E

Tree Finder
1925-1927

Home Nurse
1924-1927

Brown Owl
pin, 1927

Tawny Owl
pin, 1927

Land Scout
1920-1927

Adult uniform for a
Brown Owl (Brownie
Captain). Instead of
the trefoil pin worn
by non-Brownie
officers, the Captain
wore a Brown Owl
pin on her tie.
(Brownie lieutenants
wore the Tawny Owl
pin.) Bronze GS
collar pins were
alternatives to the
embroidered GS
fabric squares. Both
fabric and leather
belts were official
with this uniform.
Beginning in 1918,
Lieutenants through
District Leaders wore
one to four stripes at
their left sleeve cuff
to indicate rank.
The two stripes
here indicate a
Captain/Brown Owl.

All-wool French
crepe "flapper style"
dress in pearl grey
with garnet satin
collar, tie, and cuffs.
Felt cloche hat.

Peacetime wedding dress in
satin with lace sleeves and ruffles
cascading down the skirt.
Coronet headpiece of Brussels
lace with tulle veil.

Rock Tapper
1920-1925

Hostess
1920-1927

Scout
Entertainer
1920-1922

Woodcraft
Scout
1928-1938

Journalist
1928-1938

Motorist
1928-1938

Brownie uniform
proposed but
never made
official.

Golden Hand
Award, 1926
The Brownie
sign was made
with two fingers
held up.

Raglan-sleeved
wool coat and
felt hat. Collar,
cuffs, and
pockets trimmed
with embroidery.

First official Brownie
uniform. The Golden
Bar on pocket bottom
was earned by younger
Brownies; the Golden
Hand above the pocket,
by older Brownies.
The Six emblem
served in place
of a patrol crest
and matched
the tabs on the
right shoulder.
The hat always
folded over to the
right.

Brownie Pin,
1926

Girl Scout
Neighbor
1928-1938

Brownie Wings,
1926
Brownie wings
appeared on
only a Girl
Scout's uniform
to show she had
been a Brownie.

International
Knowledge
1928-1931

Star Finder
1928-1938

Garden Flower
Finder
1928-1938

Girl Scout Aide
1928-1938

Tenderfoot
pin, 1923-1934

Interpreter
1928-1931

Girl's uniform
skirt with elastic
waistband, worn
with a Girl Scout
middy blouse.
Suitable for all
outdoor
activities, it could
be worn over
bloomers for
hiking.
Introduced in
the 1928 catalog
as an official
uniform option,
in 1929 it was
termed camp
wear, not an
official uniform.

First green uniform for
girls. Background fabric
on badges and the
armband also changed to
green. Black embroidery
changed to dark green.
The Scholarship award
was introduced in 1922
and worn only on the left
sleeve. The GS insignia
was embroidered directly
onto the collar. Patrol
Leader chevrons point
up for the first time.
The silver stripe
indicates five years
membership service;
later, gold indicated
ten years. For each
time an annual badge
was earned, a different
colored ring was
embroidered around
it.

First green
uniform for
adults. Adult
position stripes
changed to dark
green, and
collars of various
colors still
denoted some
positions
(neither
pertained to Mrs.
Hoover at this
time). With the
adult tie
eliminated, the
pin was worn
directly on the
uniform.

Dancer
1928-1938

Camp Edith
Macy pin, 1926

Rock Finder
1928-1938

Athlete
1928-1938

Our whole patrol is working on the Electrician and Telegrapher proficiency badges. Each of us is making a practice telegraph sending pad. We were all inspired by Margaret's ability with Morse Code in *The Golden Eaglet*, and we want to "Be Prepared," too! My Daddy says he is just grateful I'm learning how to replace burnt-out fuses, so he can have help with that particular task at home!

January 27, 1922: Miss Daisy has been having a wonderful time entertaining everyone who is here in Savannah for the National Convention. She used her famous secret family recipe to make waffles for some of the national staff, and of course they loved them. Mrs. Herbert Hoover (her given name is "Lou Henry"—isn't that an unusually lovely combination?) was elected President of Girl Scouts, and Miss Daisy was most particularly pleased about that.

Melissa has told me about the plans to send two girls from Georgia to Camp Andree Clark in Westchester County in the hills of New York. Actually, EVERY state is sending two girls to this first camp there, but we were discussing the fact that she is *too old* and I am *too young* to be chosen as one of the campers. TOO BAD! We have heard through Miss Daisy's "grapevine" that the pin for the camp is going to be shaped like a feather with the initials C.A.C. on it. Sounds pretty. Melissa is getting excited as the time gets closer for her to be able to wear GOLD service stripes on her uniform, showing she has been a Girl Scout for ten whole years!

September 17, 1922: Melissa came by today, all excited about an article in *Field News*, the new magazine for leaders. The very first issue was last April, and she says the articles have been a great help to her. She was also wishing she could attend the first American Brownie Pow-Wow, to be held in November in Norbeck, Maryland. It seems that many leaders across the country are expecting some definite decisions and statements from this Pow-Wow concerning uniforms and programs. I hope the Brownie idea grows; I remember thinking I might just DIE before I got old enough to be a Girl Scout!

Last spring, I was reading in our handbook about the "land army" of the French Girl Scouts (called Eclaireuses)—girls who did their part to help their country by raising wonderful vegetable crops. I suggested to my Captain that our troop could be of true help to our community by raising vegetables to give to those who could not afford to buy them. We hoped it might also provide a "crop" of money to buy more seeds for next year and supplies to make Christmas gifts for the needy families we help each year. It is working even better than we dreamed. We are still harvesting vegetables and continuing our record-keeping. The whole troop is earning the Gardener proficiency badge as we work on this. We planted a flower border around the edges of our garden plot and have taken the cut blooms to hospitals and invalids and also to some of the people who have been especially helpful to all the Girl Scouts of Savannah over the years. Daddy calls us his perennial "flower girls."

The American Girl also had a suggestion for money-earning that appealed to our troop: selling "Girl Scout made" cookies. We will definitely use this idea, as soon as we can agree on what kind to make!

We can now earn a Community Service Award. It takes the place of the old War Service Award. It, too, is based on points received for canning, food production, farming, hospital assistance, and work with other service organizations.

November 15, 1924: For the second year in a row, Daisy Low wrote a message to all Girl Scouts on her Halloween birthday. It was printed in *The American Girl*. She really is an inspiration to "her girls"—US!

I believe I have gotten my wish about the Brownies. The Pow-Wow set up a suggested uniform and basic program to help the Brown Owl (Captain) and the Tawny Owl (Lieutenant). This year, Miss Edith Ballinger Price has written a pamphlet of information to be mailed to those wishing to organize a Brownie pack.

The World Camp and International Conference was held this past summer at Foxlease, in New Forest, England. Miss Daisy has been telling us for two years about the fun she's had getting her cottage ready there. The land for the camp was given to British Girl Guides by an American woman, Mrs. Anne Archbold. One cottage was to be Miss Daisy's to decorate just for entertaining Girl Guides and Girl Scouts from all over the world. Daisy named it "The Link," to symbolize the bond between the Girl Guides and the Girl Scouts. The tale is now told that The Link had the only bathtub in camp, and girls were invited by Daisy to use it any time, an invitation which frequently extended to their staying for breakfast!

December 28, 1925: I received the most wonderful Christmas present: a book called *Girl Scout Short Stories*. It has taken all my Girl Scout training to make me help around the house as I am supposed to do and not just spend all my time reading! The stories are all ones that were winners in the annual "What-I-Wish-in-My-Magazine" contest in *The American Girl*. There are also wonderful poems reprinted from other publications, and even a whole section on "Things Girls Like to Make" (a wren house, a woodsy picture frame, a rustic fern basket, and a camp memory book—I intend to make one of these for my cousin and one for myself). So far, my favorite story is "The Lone Scout Who Wasn't Lonely." I had read in our handbook about the idea of Lone Scouts (girls who live in areas too sparsely populated to allow formation of troops, but who want to be a Girl Scout and earn badges and be a part of the Movement), and this story shows the beautiful way other people respond to befriend Girl Scouts anywhere.

December 30, 1926: Wow! What an exciting year this has been!

Last February, the city of Savannah honored our beloved Juliette Gordon Low at a ceremony by the fountain in Forsythe Park. She received a scroll from the city, and Girl Scouts presented her with an elegant silver tea and coffee service.

My favorite statement of the day was the telegram from Mrs. Jane Deeter Rippin of the national organization, describing our Founder this way: "She had the heart to resolve, the head to contrive, and the hand to execute."

The national headquarters has issued a leader's guide for Brownie Girl Scout leaders, the *Brown Book for Brown Owls*. I have read through some of it, and I know girls are going to love its "magic," such as the idea of the Golden Ground on which a Brownie stands, ready to lend a hand. My little cousin, Lois, is so proud of being elected the Sixer (leader) of her Six (patrol)! As the Sixer, she gets to have red shoulder tabs to match the red embroidery on the emblem chosen by their Six, the Leprechaun. They are enjoying taking care of the plot we gave them in the corner of our troop garden. To earn the rank of Golden Bar, younger Brownies feed and observe pets, carve two articles, or throw and catch a ball from ten yards away. (I am now working on a similar requirement for my Athlete proficiency badge, demonstrating accurate baseball pitching from a distance of *forty* feet. Thanks to the hours I have spent playing baseball with my brothers Brandon and Ryan, this is easy for me!) Older Brownies may earn the Golden Hand by doing activities such as finding the North Star and another constellation, cooking a simple dish, knowing how to clean and bandage a finger, and make change from a dollar.

Last summer, Miss Daisy's fondest wish came true: the fourth World Conference was held at the VERY newly completed Camp Edith Macy in New York State. (Melissa said Doots told her that the last of the workmen literally went out the back door of the Great Hall as the delegates came in the front door!) There were fifty-six foreign delegates and four hundred U.S. delegates. Sir Baden-Powell and Lady Baden-Powell were both there; in fact, Miss Daisy and Lady Baden-Powell led the motorcade from New York City out to the wooded acres of Camp Macy. At the opening that night of both Camp Edith Macy and the World Conference, delegates spoke eloquently of the special gifts their countries brought to the world. Delegates received a pin in the shape of a lamp of knowledge, with the letters "C.E.M." (for Camp Edith Macy) superimposed on it, plus a Tenderfoot pin (unearned!) engraved with a "W" (for the World Conference). One of the ideas that came from this conference was for a special day to be set aside for Girl Guides and Girl Scouts to think about all their sisters in the Movement throughout the world. The date selected was February 22, the birthday of BOTH Sir Robert and Lady Olave Baden-Powell.

Thinking about all Miss Daisy has done almost made me not write down the comparatively trifling feat of passing the proficiency tests for my Scout Aide badge last winter. But then I realized that Miss Daisy's example is one of learning and keeping on learning. She has always been proud of every single accomplishment any Girl Scout ever reported. I have worked and worked and worked to earn the six necessary badges: First Aide, Home Nurse, Homemaker, Health Winner, Health Guardian, and Child Nurse. Then the National Headquarters had to approve all I had done before I could receive my badge. I really needed to know lots of this when Nonna was so ill all this past year. I actually knew more to do to help with Nonna than Mother did! I knew how and what to cook for invalids, how to make poultices, how to make flaxseed

tea for her cough, how to air a room, and much more. As sick as she was, Nonna noticed and complimented me on the quality of my care. She thought I did an especially good job of making the bed with her in it. Our handbook requires that this be done in fifteen minutes. I got to the point I could do it in only EIGHT, and without stirring up Nonna's aches and pains. The best news is that she's well now!

January 18, 1927: I have cried until my head hurts. Miss Daisy died yesterday and will be buried at Laurel Grove Cemetery. It's so hard to believe she will never go camping with us again, never tell another story around the campfire, never laugh with us. I keep telling myself that what I must remember is all the good times we DID have. She has, after all, left behind the very best of herself—that part that she put into giving us Girl Scouting. Now we shall keep it going for her. At her request, she was buried in her uniform. In the pocket was the telegram she received from her friends at National Headquarters: "You are not only the first Girl Scout, you are the best Girl Scout of them all."

October 31, 1927: Miss Daisy would have been sixty-seven years old today. We miss her every day, but her organization has certainly kept growing in a way that would have pleased her deeply. Last June, a shortened version of the handbook was published, removing all war emphasis and references. Girl Scouting seems to work hard to be up-to-date.

The first United States Girl Scout Troops on Foreign Soil (TOFS for short) were registered this year. Miss Daisy spent so much of her adult life in England, and loved traveling so much, that this is an idea she would have loved.

Several troops got together for a "Remembering Miss Daisy" campout last weekend. While we went hiking down some of Miss Daisy's favorite paths, we left our evening meal in Norwegian Fireless Cookers, the kind we learned to make from our handbook. (It took two to feed all of us.) For each one, we used a one-gallon agate pail with a tight-fitting lid. We put in our boiling stew, then set each pail into a wooden case we had made (the required eight inches larger all around than the pail). We packed around one pail with paper and around the second one with the ground cork Malaga grapes are packed in for shipping, pressing a cushion of packing on top as well as around the sides, and fastening the lid down tightly. As always, it worked perfectly.

We also made our old favorite, lemonade powder, to take with us. (This is made by heavily sweetening pure lemon juice and then letting all the moisture evaporate over several days. The residue is crumbled and packed in gelatin capsules. For lemonade in a hurry, drop one or more capsules into a cup of water and stir well.)

We saw many of Miss Daisy's favorite kinds of birds as we walked, thanks to the nesting boxes, bird baths, and feeding stations we learned to make when we all joined the Audubon Society as our handbook suggested. Through this we have followed the plight of certain birds, and we are all glad that it is now against the law to wear or

even possess egret plumes. Birds shouldn't have to die just to decorate a lady's hat!

Being out-of-doors, using the skills Miss Daisy taught us, and remembering our favorite times with her brought her close in our memories.

October 27, 1928: Girl Scouts have a new uniform! Of a new color: a gray-green! It is very stylish, short, and with a wonderful four-gored, crushable soft-crown hat of the same fabric. I especially like the pleats on the sides and in the back. They let the dress hang in a fashionably slim, straight line, while still providing the fullness needed for moving about. Green may become THE Girl Scout color. New badges will be on the gray-green fabric, with dark green borders and with all previously black embroidery now done in dark green. With my bobbed hair, I will look a perfectly acceptable flapper in my new uniform! (Now if I could just learn the "turkey trot"! I know WORLDS of steps to the "Charleston.")

At the meeting in Hungary this past summer, the International Council officially became known as the World Association of Girl Guides and Girl Scouts (already known, for the sake of convenience, as WAGGGS—pronounced "wags"). A World Bureau has been set up and a World Committee formed. *The World Bulletin*, which began publication in 1925, changed its name last year to *The Council Fire.* I think Melissa subscribes.

Two very excellent ideas have developed to honor our Miss Daisy. The Juliette Low World Friendship Fund has been established. It is most appropriate that contributions to it will support projects and events promoting international friendship and understanding. Also, Miss Daisy's October 31 birthday will be known as Founder's Day, and Girl Scouts by the thousands, literally around the globe, will gather to remember and honor her on this day.

We are having a special celebration of Founder's Day, with a pot luck supper and a style show of new and old uniforms. Betty (Melissa's big sister) will model her Brown Owl uniform. She has loved her first year of working with her daughter's Brownie pack. She will also wear a Lieutenant's uniform from 1912, the year Miss Daisy started Girl Scouts. We are so fortunate that the uniform's owner is still active with the Movement and was tickled pink to loan the uniform for this Founder's Day show. My little cousin, Lois, will wear two Brownie uniforms. The first is her own, which is the very first official one; the other is one of the "trial" styles some groups experimented with back in 1918. It is khaki. I'm so glad they finally decided on brown for the official uniform; it seems only logical for a Brownie!

I am to wear one of the new green uniform dresses for girls, and our Captain will wear her new green adult uniform (I understand Mrs. Hoover has one of these also). We will be the fashion hit of the show! I will also wear the camp middy and skirt which is part of the new uniform. For those of us who like to camp as much as Miss Daisy did, this uniform option is a pretty good idea—it lets us cut down on the number of uniform pieces we need.

And so, as I leave for my troop's Founder's Day festivities, I will salute and say, "Happy Birthday, Juliette Gordon 'Daisy' Low! And from ALL your Girl Scouts, THANK YOU!!"

Girl Guide Laws 1912

1. A Guide's Honour Is to Be Trusted.
2. A Guide Is Loyal.
3. A Guide's Duty Is to Be Useful and to Help Others.
4. A Guide Is a Friend to All, and a Sister to Every Other Guide, no matter to what Social Class the Other Belongs.
5. A Guide Is Courteous.
6. A Guide Keeps Herself Pure in Thoughts, Words, and Deeds.
7. A Guide Is a Friend to Animals.
8. A Guide Obeys Orders.
9. A Guide Smiles and Sings.
10. A Guide Is Thrifty.

Girl Scout Laws 1913

1. A Girl Scout's Honor Is to Be Trusted.
2. A Girl Scout Is Loyal.
3. A Girl Scout's Duty Is to Be Useful and to Help Others.
4. A Girl Scout Is a Friend to All, and a Sister to Every Other Girl Scout no Matter to what Social Class she May Belong.
5. A Girl Scout Is Courteous.
6. A Girl Scout Keeps Herself Pure.
7. A Girl Scout Is a Friend to Animals.
8. A Girl Scout Obeys Orders.
9. A Girl Scout Is Cheerful.
10. A Girl Scout Is Thrifty.

Girl Scout Laws 1920

1. A Girl Scout's Honor Is to Be Trusted.
2. A Girl Scout Is Loyal.
3. A Girl Scout's Duty Is to Be Useful and to Help Others.
4. A Girl Scout Is a Friend to All, and a Sister to Every Other Girl Scout.
5. A Girl Scout Is Courteous.
6. A Girl Scout Is a Friend to Animals.
7. A Girl Scout Obeys Orders.
8. A Girl Scout Is Cheerful.
9. A Girl Scout Is Thrifty.
10. A Girl Scout Is Clean in Thought, Word, and Deed.

References

Baden-Powell, Agnes. *The Handbook for Girl Guides or How Girls Can Help Build the Empire.* London: Thomas Nelson and Sons, 1910.

Baden-Powell, Olave, Lady G.B.E., as told to Mary Drewery. *Window on My Heart.* London: Cox and Wyman Limited, 1973.

Blum, Stella, ed. *Everyday Fashions of the Twenties as Pictured in Sears and Other Catalogs.* New York: Dover Press, 1981.

Choate, Anne Hyde, and Helen Ferris. *Juliette Low and the Girl Scouts.* New York: Doubleday, Page and Company, 1928.

Degenhardt, Mary. "How Brownies Came to Be Brownie Girl Scouts." *Girl Scout Leader*, Spring, 1993.

Degenhardt, Mary, and Judith Kirsch. *Girl Scout Collector's Guide.* Lombard, Ill.: Wallace-Homestead Book Company, 1987.

The Delineator. February, 1921.

Encyclopaedia Britannica. Chicago: Helen Hemingway Benton, 1976.

Girl Scout Short Stories. New York: Doubleday, Page and Company, 1925.

Girl Scout Uniforms through the Years. New York: Girl Scouts of the U.S.A., 1986.

Hillcourt, William. *Baden-Powell: The Two Lives of a Hero, 80th Birthday Edition.* Irving, Tex.: Boy Scouts of America, 1964; reprint, 1981.

Hoxie, Walter John. *How Girls Can Help Their Country.* Washington, D.C.: Girl Scouts of the U.S.A., 1913; reprint, 1972.

Ladies' Home Journal. March, 1912; September, 1919.

McCall's Magazine. July, 1925.

Montgomery Ward and Company Catalog. Fort Worth, Spring and Summer, 1925.

National Cloak and Suit Company Catalog. 1912.

Pace, Mildred Mastin. *Juliette Low.* New York: Charles Scribner's Sons, 1947.

Radford, Ruby L. *Juliette Low, Girl Scout Founder.* Champaign, Ill.: Garrard Publishing Company, 1965.

Schroeder, Joseph J., Jr., ed. *The Wonderful World of Ladies' Fashion.* Chicago: Digest Books, 1971.

Scouting For Girls. New York: Girl Scouts, Incorporated, 1920; fifth reprint, 1924.

Sears, Roebuck and Company Catalog. Chicago, Spring, 1912; Spring, 1918.

75 Years of Girl Scouting. New York: Girl Scouts of the U.S.A., 1986.

Willett, C., and Phillis Cunnington. *The History of Underclothes.* New York: Dover Press, 1992.

Women's and Children's Fashions of 1917, The Complete Perry, Dame and Company Catalog, Spring and Summer, 1917. New York: Dover Press, 1992.

World Book Encyclopedia. Chicago: Field Enterprises Educational Corporation, 1974.

Glossary

Baden-Powell (bay'den pole), *Agnes*—author of the first Girl Guide handbook and sister of Robert Baden-Powell.

Baden-Powell, Lady Olave—wife of Robert Baden-Powell, elected World Chief Guide in 1930.

Baden-Powell, Sir Robert—founder of both Boy Scouts and Girl Guides; honored by King George of England with a peerage, becoming Lord Baden-Powell of Gilwell in 1929.

badge—in the first Girl Guide and Girl Scout handbooks, the word had a dual meaning. "Trefoil badge" or "brooch" meant what is now called a membership pin. Used alone, it referred to the embroidered symbol to be worn on the uniform to represent an area of knowledge gained. Originally, badges were awarded by "proficiency tests for badges." Then, in the 1920 handbook, they were called "merit badges," the name used by Boy Scouts. The name soon evolved to "proficiency badges," which remains today.

bretelles—suspender-like band trimming for dress bodice or blouse, extending from shoulder to waist on front and back.

Brown Owl—Brownie Captain (leader).

Brussels lace—needle-point lace made with corded, separate designs appliqued to fine net.

Captain—original title for troop leader.

chevron—stripe motif consisting of two lines forming an inverted V, usually signifying rank.

chiffon—delicately sheer, open-weaved fabric of cotton, silk, rayon, or synthetics, soft or stiff in finish; for dresses, blouses, night wear, or scarves.

company—original name for troop; made up of two or more patrols.

crepe de chine—lustrous lightweight silk or rayon, slightly crinkled or crepe-like in texture, for dresses and blouses.

fichu—ruffly or shawl-like draping on shoulders and bosom of dress or blouse.

Gabrielle—daytime dress with large box pleats on each side.

Girl Scouts of the U.S.A.—correct name for the Girl Scout organization today. In the earliest days, it was simply called The Girl Scouts, then Girl Scouts, Inc.

investiture—ceremony at which a girl officially says her Promise and receives her Girl Scout membership pin.

knickerbockers—for women, bloomers named for Dietrick Knickerbocker, a fictional character created by American author Washington Irving; originally referring to baggy knee breeches worn by men and boys from the 1860s on.

lawn—A sheer plainwoven cotton or linen fabric that is given various finishes (such as semicrisp) when used for clothing.

Lieutenant—original name for assistant troop leader.

middy—sailor blouse or dress with a collar that usually hangs square in the back and tapers in the front to a V with a loop through which a sailor tie is slipped.

moiré—stiff, heavy ribbed fabric of rayon or acetate and cotton, embossed for a watered look; for evening wear and accessories.

nainsook—a soft, lightweight, bleached cotton, lustrous on one side; for lingerie and infants clothing.

Norfolk jacket—belted, singlebreasted jacket, pleated from shoulder to hem, front and back, with slots under pleats through which belt is threaded.

organdy—sheer open-weaved cotton with permanently crisp finish; for dresses, aprons, collars, cuffs and millinery.

passementerie—trimmings, especially heay embroideries or rich edgings of braids, beads, lace, silks, etc.

patrol—governmental division within a troop/company. In the early days, patrols were much more self-contained than they are today. A Patrol Leader is the elected or appointed leader of the group.

percale—smooth, lightweight, plain-weaved cotton fabric; for dresses, shirts, children's clothing, and sheeting.

piqué—firm, double-woven fabrics, usually cotton, with crosswise corded ribs or honeycomb or diamond weaves.

Plauen lace—lace embroidered on a background fabric, which is then chemically burned or dissolved away, leaving only the lace designs.

point de Paris lace—narrow bobbin lace with hexagonal mesh and flat design.

princess slip—fitted slip of flared or straight vertical panels with no waistline seam.

Sixer—leader of the Brownie Six (patrol).

tatting—knotted, usually narrow lace, made with the fingers and a hand-held shuttle, for edging lingerie and handkerchiefs.

Tawny Owl—Brownie Lieutenant.

trefoil—three-leaved shape of the Girl Scout pin and logo, representing the three parts of the Girl Scout Promise.

tulle—fine sheer net of silk, nylon, or rayon, with hexagonal holes; used unstarched for bridal veils and millinery and starched for ballet costumes.

Valenciennes lace—fine, flat French bobbin lace of linen; handmade, with the same threads forming small floral and bow designs and a background of square, diamond-shaped, or round mesh.

even possess egret plumes. Birds shouldn't have to die just to decorate a lady's hat!

Being out-of-doors, using the skills Miss Daisy taught us, and remembering our favorite times with her brought her close in our memories.

October 27, 1928: Girl Scouts have a new uniform! Of a new color: a gray-green! It is very stylish, short, and with a wonderful four-gored, crushable soft-crown hat of the same fabric. I especially like the pleats on the sides and in the back. They let the dress hang in a fashionably slim, straight line, while still providing the fullness needed for moving about. Green may become THE Girl Scout color. New badges will be on the gray-green fabric, with dark green borders and with all previously black embroidery now done in dark green. With my bobbed hair, I will look a perfectly acceptable flapper in my new uniform! (Now if I could just learn the "turkey trot"! I know WORLDS of steps to the "Charleston.")

At the meeting in Hungary this past summer, the International Council officially became known as the World Association of Girl Guides and Girl Scouts (already known, for the sake of convenience, as WAGGGS—pronounced "wags"). A World Bureau has been set up and a World Committee formed. *The World Bulletin*, which began publication in 1925, changed its name last year to *The Council Fire.* I think Melissa subscribes.

Two very excellent ideas have developed to honor our Miss Daisy. The Juliette Low World Friendship Fund has been established. It is most appropriate that contributions to it will support projects and events promoting international friendship and understanding. Also, Miss Daisy's October 31 birthday will be known as Founder's Day, and Girl Scouts by the thousands, literally around the globe, will gather to remember and honor her on this day.

We are having a special celebration of Founder's Day, with a pot luck supper and a style show of new and old uniforms. Betty (Melissa's big sister) will model her Brown Owl uniform. She has loved her first year of working with her daughter's Brownie pack. She will also wear a Lieutenant's uniform from 1912, the year Miss Daisy started Girl Scouts. We are so fortunate that the uniform's owner is still active with the Movement and was tickled pink to loan the uniform for this Founder's Day show. My little cousin, Lois, will wear two Brownie uniforms. The first is her own, which is the very first official one; the other is one of the "trial" styles some groups experimented with back in 1918. It is khaki. I'm so glad they finally decided on brown for the official uniform; it seems only logical for a Brownie!

I am to wear one of the new green uniform dresses for girls, and our Captain will wear her new green adult uniform (I understand Mrs. Hoover has one of these also). We will be the fashion hit of the show! I will also wear the camp middy and skirt which is part of the new uniform. For those of us who like to camp as much as Miss Daisy did, this uniform option is a pretty good idea—it lets us cut down on the number of uniform pieces we need.

And so, as I leave for my troop's Founder's Day festivities, I will salute and say, "Happy Birthday, Juliette Gordon 'Daisy' Low! And from ALL your Girl Scouts, THANK YOU!!"

Girl Guide Laws 1912

1. A Guide's Honour Is to Be Trusted.
2. A Guide Is Loyal.
3. A Guide's Duty Is to Be Useful and to Help Others.
4. A Guide Is a Friend to All, and a Sister to Every Other Guide, no matter to what Social Class the Other Belongs.
5. A Guide Is Courteous.
6. A Guide Keeps Herself Pure in Thoughts, Words, and Deeds.
7. A Guide Is a Friend to Animals.
8. A Guide Obeys Orders.
9. A Guide Smiles and Sings.
10. A Guide Is Thrifty.

Girl Scout Laws 1913

1. A Girl Scout's Honor Is to Be Trusted.
2. A Girl Scout Is Loyal.
3. A Girl Scout's Duty Is to Be Useful and to Help Others.
4. A Girl Scout Is a Friend to All, and a Sister to Every Other Girl Scout no Matter to what Social Class she May Belong.
5. A Girl Scout Is Courteous.
6. A Girl Scout Keeps Herself Pure.
7. A Girl Scout Is a Friend to Animals.
8. A Girl Scout Obeys Orders.
9. A Girl Scout Is Cheerful.
10. A Girl Scout Is Thrifty.

Girl Scout Laws 1920

1. A Girl Scout's Honor Is to Be Trusted.
2. A Girl Scout Is Loyal.
3. A Girl Scout's Duty Is to Be Useful and to Help Others.
4. A Girl Scout Is a Friend to All, and a Sister to Every Other Girl Scout.
5. A Girl Scout Is Courteous.
6. A Girl Scout Is a Friend to Animals.
7. A Girl Scout Obeys Orders.
8. A Girl Scout Is Cheerful.
9. A Girl Scout Is Thrifty.
10. A Girl Scout Is Clean in Thought, Word, and Deed.

References

Baden-Powell, Agnes. *The Handbook for Girl Guides or How Girls Can Help Build the Empire.* London: Thomas Nelson and Sons, 1910.

Baden-Powell, Olave, Lady G.B.E., as told to Mary Drewery. *Window on My Heart.* London: Cox and Wyman Limited, 1973.

Blum, Stella, ed. *Everyday Fashions of the Twenties as Pictured in Sears and Other Catalogs.* New York: Dover Press, 1981.

Choate, Anne Hyde, and Helen Ferris. *Juliette Low and the Girl Scouts.* New York: Doubleday, Page and Company, 1928.

Degenhardt, Mary. "How Brownies Came to Be Brownie Girl Scouts." *Girl Scout Leader*, Spring, 1993.

Degenhardt, Mary, and Judith Kirsch. *Girl Scout Collector's Guide.* Lombard, Ill.: Wallace-Homestead Book Company, 1987.

The Delineator. February, 1921.

Encyclopaedia Britannica. Chicago: Helen Hemingway Benton, 1976.

Girl Scout Short Stories. New York: Doubleday, Page and Company, 1925.

Girl Scout Uniforms through the Years. New York: Girl Scouts of the U.S.A., 1986.

Hillcourt, William. *Baden-Powell: The Two Lives of a Hero, 80th Birthday Edition.* Irving, Tex.: Boy Scouts of America, 1964; reprint, 1981.

Hoxie, Walter John. *How Girls Can Help Their Country.* Washington, D.C.: Girl Scouts of the U.S.A., 1913; reprint, 1972.

Ladies' Home Journal. March, 1912; September, 1919.

McCall's Magazine. July, 1925.

Montgomery Ward and Company Catalog. Fort Worth, Spring and Summer, 1925.

National Cloak and Suit Company Catalog. 1912.

Pace, Mildred Mastin. *Juliette Low.* New York: Charles Scribner's Sons, 1947.

Radford, Ruby L. *Juliette Low, Girl Scout Founder.* Champaign, Ill.: Garrard Publishing Company, 1965.

Schroeder, Joseph J., Jr., ed. *The Wonderful World of Ladies' Fashion.* Chicago: Digest Books, 1971.

Scouting For Girls. New York: Girl Scouts, Incorporated, 1920; fifth reprint, 1924.

Sears, Roebuck and Company Catalog. Chicago, Spring, 1912; Spring, 1918.

75 Years of Girl Scouting. New York: Girl Scouts of the U.S.A., 1986.

Willett, C., and Phillis Cunnington. *The History of Underclothes.* New York: Dover Press, 1992.

Women's and Children's Fashions of 1917, The Complete Perry, Dame and Company Catalog, Spring and Summer, 1917. New York: Dover Press, 1992.

World Book Encyclopedia. Chicago: Field Enterprises Educational Corporation, 1974.

Glossary

Baden-Powell (bay'den pole), *Agnes*—author of the first Girl Guide handbook and sister of Robert Baden-Powell.

Baden-Powell, Lady Olave—wife of Robert Baden-Powell, elected World Chief Guide in 1930.

Baden-Powell, Sir Robert—founder of both Boy Scouts and Girl Guides; honored by King George of England with a peerage, becoming Lord Baden-Powell of Gilwell in 1929.

badge—in the first Girl Guide and Girl Scout handbooks, the word had a dual meaning. "Trefoil badge" or "brooch" meant what is now called a membership pin. Used alone, it referred to the embroidered symbol to be worn on the uniform to represent an area of knowledge gained. Originally, badges were awarded by "proficiency tests for badges." Then, in the 1920 handbook, they were called "merit badges," the name used by Boy Scouts. The name soon evolved to "proficiency badges," which remains today.

bretelles—suspender-like band trimming for dress bodice or blouse, extending from shoulder to waist on front and back.

Brown Owl—Brownie Captain (leader).

Brussels lace—needle-point lace made with corded, separate designs appliqued to fine net.

Captain—original title for troop leader.

chevron—stripe motif consisting of two lines forming an inverted V, usually signifying rank.

chiffon—delicately sheer, open-weaved fabric of cotton, silk, rayon, or synthetics, soft or stiff in finish; for dresses, blouses, night wear, or scarves.

company—original name for troop; made up of two or more patrols.

crepe de chine—lustrous lightweight silk or rayon, slightly crinkled or crepe-like in texture, for dresses and blouses.

fichu—ruffly or shawl-like draping on shoulders and bosom of dress or blouse.

Gabrielle—daytime dress with large box pleats on each side.

Girl Scouts of the U.S.A.—correct name for the Girl Scout organization today. In the earliest days, it was simply called The Girl Scouts, then Girl Scouts, Inc.

investiture—ceremony at which a girl officially says her Promise and receives her Girl Scout membership pin.

knickerbockers—for women, bloomers named for Dietrick Knickerbocker, a fictional character created by American author Washington Irving; originally referring to baggy knee breeches worn by men and boys from the 1860s on.

lawn—A sheer plainwoven cotton or linen fabric that is given various finishes (such as semicrisp) when used for clothing.

Lieutenant—original name for assistant troop leader.

middy—sailor blouse or dress with a collar that usually hangs square in the back and tapers in the front to a V with a loop through which a sailor tie is slipped.

moiré—stiff, heavy ribbed fabric of rayon or acetate and cotton, embossed for a watered look; for evening wear and accessories.

nainsook—a soft, lightweight, bleached cotton, lustrous on one side; for lingerie and infants clothing.

Norfolk jacket—belted, singlebreasted jacket, pleated from shoulder to hem, front and back, with slots under pleats through which belt is threaded.

organdy—sheer open-weaved cotton with permanently crisp finish; for dresses, aprons, collars, cuffs and millinery.

passementerie—trimmings, especially heay embroideries or rich edgings of braids, beads, lace, silks, etc.

patrol—governmental division within a troop/company. In the early days, patrols were much more self-contained than they are today. A Patrol Leader is the elected or appointed leader of the group.

percale—smooth, lightweight, plain-weaved cotton fabric; for dresses, shirts, children's clothing, and sheeting.

piqué—firm, double-woven fabrics, usually cotton, with crosswise corded ribs or honeycomb or diamond weaves.

Plauen lace—lace embroidered on a background fabric, which is then chemically burned or dissolved away, leaving only the lace designs.

point de Paris lace—narrow bobbin lace with hexagonal mesh and flat design.

princess slip—fitted slip of flared or straight vertical panels with no waistline seam.

Sixer—leader of the Brownie Six (patrol).

tatting—knotted, usually narrow lace, made with the fingers and a hand-held shuttle, for edging lingerie and handkerchiefs.

Tawny Owl—Brownie Lieutenant.

trefoil—three-leaved shape of the Girl Scout pin and logo, representing the three parts of the Girl Scout Promise.

tulle—fine sheer net of silk, nylon, or rayon, with hexagonal holes; used unstarched for bridal veils and millinery and starched for ballet costumes.

Valenciennes lace—fine, flat French bobbin lace of linen; handmade, with the same threads forming small floral and bow designs and a background of square, diamond-shaped, or round mesh.

even possess egret plumes. Birds shouldn't have to die just to decorate a lady's hat!

Being out-of-doors, using the skills Miss Daisy taught us, and remembering our favorite times with her brought her close in our memories.

October 27, 1928: Girl Scouts have a new uniform! Of a new color: a gray-green! It is very stylish, short, and with a wonderful four-gored, crushable soft-crown hat of the same fabric. I especially like the pleats on the sides and in the back. They let the dress hang in a fashionably slim, straight line, while still providing the fullness needed for moving about. Green may become THE Girl Scout color. New badges will be on the gray-green fabric, with dark green borders and with all previously black embroidery now done in dark green. With my bobbed hair, I will look a perfectly acceptable flapper in my new uniform! (Now if I could just learn the "turkey trot"! I know WORLDS of steps to the "Charleston.")

At the meeting in Hungary this past summer, the International Council officially became known as the World Association of Girl Guides and Girl Scouts (already known, for the sake of convenience, as WAGGGS— pronounced "wags"). A World Bureau has been set up and a World Committee formed. *The World Bulletin*, which began publication in 1925, changed its name last year to *The Council Fire.* I think Melissa subscribes.

Two very excellent ideas have developed to honor our Miss Daisy. The Juliette Low World Friendship Fund has been established. It is most appropriate that contributions to it will support projects and events promoting international friendship and understanding. Also, Miss Daisy's October 31 birthday will be known as Founder's Day, and Girl Scouts by the thousands, literally around the globe, will gather to remember and honor her on this day.

We are having a special celebration of Founder's Day, with a pot luck supper and a style show of new and old uniforms. Betty (Melissa's big sister) will model her Brown Owl uniform. She has loved her first year of working with her daughter's Brownie pack. She will also wear a Lieutenant's uniform from 1912, the year Miss Daisy started Girl Scouts. We are so fortunate that the uniform's owner is still active with the Movement and was tickled pink to loan the uniform for this Founder's Day show. My little cousin, Lois, will wear two Brownie uniforms. The first is her own, which is the very first official one; the other is one of the "trial" styles some groups experimented with back in 1918. It is khaki. I'm so glad they finally decided on brown for the official uniform; it seems only logical for a Brownie!

I am to wear one of the new green uniform dresses for girls, and our Captain will wear her new green adult uniform (I understand Mrs. Hoover has one of these also). We will be the fashion hit of the show! I will also wear the camp middy and skirt which is part of the new uniform. For those of us who like to camp as much as Miss Daisy did, this uniform option is a pretty good idea— it lets us cut down on the number of uniform pieces we need.

And so, as I leave for my troop's Founder's Day festivities, I will salute and say, "Happy Birthday, Juliette Gordon 'Daisy' Low! And from ALL your Girl Scouts, THANK YOU!!"

Girl Guide Laws 1912

1. A Guide's Honour Is to Be Trusted.
2. A Guide Is Loyal.
3. A Guide's Duty Is to Be Useful and to Help Others.
4. A Guide Is a Friend to All, and a Sister to Every Other Guide, no matter to what Social Class the Other Belongs.
5. A Guide Is Courteous.
6. A Guide Keeps Herself Pure in Thoughts, Words, and Deeds.
7. A Guide Is a Friend to Animals.
8. A Guide Obeys Orders.
9. A Guide Smiles and Sings.
10. A Guide Is Thrifty.

Girl Scout Laws 1913

1. A Girl Scout's Honor Is to Be Trusted.
2. A Girl Scout Is Loyal.
3. A Girl Scout's Duty Is to Be Useful and to Help Others.
4. A Girl Scout Is a Friend to All, and a Sister to Every Other Girl Scout no Matter to what Social Class she May Belong.
5. A Girl Scout Is Courteous.
6. A Girl Scout Keeps Herself Pure.
7. A Girl Scout Is a Friend to Animals.
8. A Girl Scout Obeys Orders.
9. A Girl Scout Is Cheerful.
10. A Girl Scout Is Thrifty.

Girl Scout Laws 1920

1. A Girl Scout's Honor Is to Be Trusted.
2. A Girl Scout Is Loyal.
3. A Girl Scout's Duty Is to Be Useful and to Help Others.
4. A Girl Scout Is a Friend to All, and a Sister to Every Other Girl Scout.
5. A Girl Scout Is Courteous.
6. A Girl Scout Is a Friend to Animals.
7. A Girl Scout Obeys Orders.
8. A Girl Scout Is Cheerful.
9. A Girl Scout Is Thrifty.
10. A Girl Scout Is Clean in Thought, Word, and Deed.

References

Baden-Powell, Agnes. *The Handbook for Girl Guides or How Girls Can Help Build the Empire.* London: Thomas Nelson and Sons, 1910.

Baden-Powell, Olave, Lady G.B.E., as told to Mary Drewery. *Window on My Heart.* London: Cox and Wyman Limited, 1973.

Blum, Stella, ed. *Everyday Fashions of the Twenties as Pictured in Sears and Other Catalogs.* New York: Dover Press, 1981.

Choate, Anne Hyde, and Helen Ferris. *Juliette Low and the Girl Scouts.* New York: Doubleday, Page and Company, 1928.

Degenhardt, Mary. "How Brownies Came to Be Brownie Girl Scouts." *Girl Scout Leader*, Spring, 1993.

Degenhardt, Mary, and Judith Kirsch. *Girl Scout Collector's Guide.* Lombard, Ill.: Wallace-Homestead Book Company, 1987.

The Delineator. February, 1921.

Encyclopaedia Britannica. Chicago: Helen Hemingway Benton, 1976.

Girl Scout Short Stories. New York: Doubleday, Page and Company, 1925.

Girl Scout Uniforms through the Years. New York: Girl Scouts of the U.S.A., 1986.

Hillcourt, William. *Baden-Powell: The Two Lives of a Hero, 80th Birthday Edition.* Irving, Tex.: Boy Scouts of America, 1964; reprint, 1981.

Hoxie, Walter John. *How Girls Can Help Their Country.* Washington, D.C.: Girl Scouts of the U.S.A., 1913; reprint, 1972.

Ladies' Home Journal. March, 1912; September, 1919.

McCall's Magazine. July, 1925.

Montgomery Ward and Company Catalog. Fort Worth, Spring and Summer, 1925.

National Cloak and Suit Company Catalog. 1912.

Pace, Mildred Mastin. *Juliette Low.* New York: Charles Scribner's Sons, 1947.

Radford, Ruby L. *Juliette Low, Girl Scout Founder.* Champaign, Ill.: Garrard Publishing Company, 1965.

Schroeder, Joseph J., Jr., ed. *The Wonderful World of Ladies' Fashion.* Chicago: Digest Books, 1971.

Scouting For Girls. New York: Girl Scouts, Incorporated, 1920; fifth reprint, 1924.

Sears, Roebuck and Company Catalog. Chicago, Spring, 1912; Spring, 1918.

75 Years of Girl Scouting. New York: Girl Scouts of the U.S.A., 1986.

Willett, C., and Phillis Cunnington. *The History of Underclothes.* New York: Dover Press, 1992.

Women's and Children's Fashions of 1917, The Complete Perry, Dame and Company Catalog, Spring and Summer, 1917. New York: Dover Press, 1992.

World Book Encyclopedia. Chicago: Field Enterprises Educational Corporation, 1974.

Glossary

Baden-Powell (bay'den pole), *Agnes*—author of the first Girl Guide handbook and sister of Robert Baden-Powell.

Baden-Powell, Lady Olave—wife of Robert Baden-Powell, elected World Chief Guide in 1930.

Baden-Powell, Sir Robert—founder of both Boy Scouts and Girl Guides; honored by King George of England with a peerage, becoming Lord Baden-Powell of Gilwell in 1929.

badge—in the first Girl Guide and Girl Scout handbooks, the word had a dual meaning. "Trefoil badge" or "brooch" meant what is now called a membership pin. Used alone, it referred to the embroidered symbol to be worn on the uniform to represent an area of knowledge gained. Originally, badges were awarded by "proficiency tests for badges." Then, in the 1920 handbook, they were called "merit badges," the name used by Boy Scouts. The name soon evolved to "proficiency badges," which remains today.

bretelles—suspender-like band trimming for dress bodice or blouse, extending from shoulder to waist on front and back.

Brown Owl—Brownie Captain (leader).

Brussels lace—needle-point lace made with corded, separate designs appliqued to fine net.

Captain—original title for troop leader.

chevron—stripe motif consisting of two lines forming an inverted V, usually signifying rank.

chiffon—delicately sheer, open-weaved fabric of cotton, silk, rayon, or synthetics, soft or stiff in finish; for dresses, blouses, night wear, or scarves.

company—original name for troop; made up of two or more patrols.

crepe de chine—lustrous lightweight silk or rayon, slightly crinkled or crepe-like in texture, for dresses and blouses.

fichu—ruffly or shawl-like draping on shoulders and bosom of dress or blouse.

Gabrielle—daytime dress with large box pleats on each side.

Girl Scouts of the U.S.A.—correct name for the Girl Scout organization today. In the earliest days, it was simply called The Girl Scouts, then Girl Scouts, Inc.

investiture—ceremony at which a girl officially says her Promise and receives her Girl Scout membership pin.

knickerbockers—for women, bloomers named for Dietrick Knickerbocker, a fictional character created by American author Washington Irving; originally referring to baggy knee breeches worn by men and boys from the 1860s on.

lawn—A sheer plainwoven cotton or linen fabric that is given various finishes (such as semicrisp) when used for clothing.

Lieutenant—original name for assistant troop leader.

middy—sailor blouse or dress with a collar that usually hangs square in the back and tapers in the front to a V with a loop through which a sailor tie is slipped.

moiré—stiff, heavy ribbed fabric of rayon or acetate and cotton, embossed for a watered look; for evening wear and accessories.

nainsook—a soft, lightweight, bleached cotton, lustrous on one side; for lingerie and infants clothing.

Norfolk jacket—belted, singlebreasted jacket, pleated from shoulder to hem, front and back, with slots under pleats through which belt is threaded.

organdy—sheer open-weaved cotton with permanently crisp finish; for dresses, aprons, collars, cuffs and millinery.

passementerie—trimmings, especially heavy embroideries or rich edgings of braids, beads, lace, silks, etc.

patrol—governmental division within a troop/company. In the early days, patrols were much more self-contained than they are today. A Patrol Leader is the elected or appointed leader of the group.

percale—smooth, lightweight, plain-weaved cotton fabric; for dresses, shirts, children's clothing, and sheeting.

piqué—firm, double-woven fabrics, usually cotton, with crosswise corded ribs or honeycomb or diamond weaves.

Plauen lace—lace embroidered on a background fabric, which is then chemically burned or dissolved away, leaving only the lace designs.

point de Paris lace—narrow bobbin lace with hexagonal mesh and flat design.

princess slip—fitted slip of flared or straight vertical panels with no waistline seam.

Sixer—leader of the Brownie Six (patrol).

tatting—knotted, usually narrow lace, made with the fingers and a hand-held shuttle, for edging lingerie and handkerchiefs.

Tawny Owl—Brownie Lieutenant.

trefoil—three-leaved shape of the Girl Scout pin and logo, representing the three parts of the Girl Scout Promise.

tulle—fine sheer net of silk, nylon, or rayon, with hexagonal holes; used unstarched for bridal veils and millinery and starched for ballet costumes.

Valenciennes lace—fine, flat French bobbin lace of linen; handmade, with the same threads forming small floral and bow designs and a background of square, diamond-shaped, or round mesh.